POEMS TO PADDLE IN

Poems to Paddle in

Compiled by Raymond Wilson

Illustrated by John Richardson

HUTCHINSON
London Sydney Auckland Johannesburg

First published in Great Britain in 1989
by Hutchinson Children's Books
An imprint of Century Hutchinson Ltd
Brookmount House, 62–65 Chandos Place,
Covent Garden, London WC2N 4NW

Century Hutchinson Australia (Pty) Ltd
88–91 Albion Street, Surry Hills, NSW 2010

Century Hutchinson New Zealand Limited
32–34 View Road, PO Box 40-086, Glenfield, Auckland 10

Century Hutchinson South Africa (Pty) Ltd
PO Box 337, Bergvlei 2012, South Africa

Printed and bound in Great Britain
Courier International Ltd, Tiptree, Essex

British Library Cataloguing in Publication Data
Poems to paddle in
I. Wilson, Raymond, 1925–
821'.914'0809282

ISBN 0-09-173963-2

Holidays

Loading of our caravan,
Lifting, dragging, carting,
Holidays, dear holidays,
Starting,
      starting,
            starting.

Weather forecast; fine and
    cool,
Salty winds are blowing.
Not a word or thought of
    school.
We're going,
      going,
          GOING!

Carnivals along the coast,
Deck chairs, coloured brollies,
Marmalade and morning toast,
Fish and chips and lollies.

Where our bounding sea dog goes,
Where the netter dabs,
Pincering the tips of toes . . .
Irritated crabs.

Bring a bucket and a spade,
Hardly time to stop,
Bands upon the promenade,
Radio and Pop.

Trips around the tossing bay,
Climbing, leaping, chasing,
How the hours will fly away,
Racing,
      racing,
          racing.

Back along the motorways,
Caravans are wending.
Holidays, dear holidays,
Ending,
      ending,
          ending.

Max Fatchen

Nowhere-in-Particular

O, Nowhere-in-Particular
Is just the place for me,
I go there every now and then
For two weeks or for three.

And Doing Nothing Special there
Is what I like to do,
At Nowhere-in-Particular
For three weeks or for two.

Colin West

I do like to be beside the seaside

Oh! I do like to be beside the seaside
I do like to be beside the sea
I do like to stroll upon the Prom, Prom, Prom,
Where the brass bands play
Tiddely om pom pom!
So just let me be beside the seaside
I'll be beside myself with glee
And there's lots of girls beside,
I should like to be beside,
Beside the seaside!
Beside the sea!

John A. Glover-Kind

6

Down to the sea

Our train stopped short; and over the fields
The children came,
Leaving their house of hay; running,
With cheeks aflame.

To cling and perch on the trackside railing —
To wave and stare:
Envying me my rockety ride
To the salt sea air.

And I waved too, and was waving still
When we moved away,
And quietly over the fields they went
To their house of hay.

Our train sped on; but left my envious
Thoughts with them there —
Wanting their play, their fields of sunshine,
And the poppies in their hair!

John Walsh

The arrival

Our train steams slowly in, and we creep to a stop at last.
There's a great unlatching of doors, and the coaches,
    emptying fast,
Let loose their loads of children, and mothers with talkative
    friends,
And sandwiches, flasks and push-chairs, and apples, and
    odds and ends.

And we move in a crowd together, amid churns and trolleys
    and crates,
Along by a cobbled courtyard, and out through the station
    gates;
We pass by the waiting taxis; then turn a corner and reach
To where with its flags and cafés the road curves down to the
    beach.

We move in the livelier air, between shining shops and stalls;
Never was such a confusion of coloured, bright beach-balls.
And plastic buckets and boats, and ducks of a rubbery blue,
And strings of sandals, and stacks of rock-with-the-name-
    right-through!

Till the many smells which beset us – of onions and cooking
    greens,
Of fumes from the cars and buses, of smoke from the noisy
    inns –
All merge in the one large gust which blows on us broad and
    free,
And catches us, throat, and limbs, and heart – the smell of
    the sea!

John Walsh

The sea

Gulls in the air –
The sea, the sea!
I saw it first!
The sea.

Shell at my ear –
The sea, the sea!
I heard it first!
The sea.

Sand in my shoe –
The sea, the sea!
I felt it first!
The sea.

Spade in my hand –
The sea, the sea!
I splashed it first!
The sea.

Cold on my toe –
The sea, the sea!
I paddled first!
The sea.

John Kitching

White horses

Far out at sea
    There are horses to ride,
Little white horses
    That race with the tide.

Their tossing manes
    Are the white sea-foam,
And the lashing winds
    Are driving them home –

To shadowy stables
    Fast they must flee,
To the great green caverns
    Down under the sea.

Irene F. Pawsey

9

Shell

I had a shell. I took my shell
and held it to my ear:
I heard the ocean sighing
far ... and far ... and near ...
I heard the seagulls crying,
and the brightness of the sea
came into Ludlow terrace
at number fifty three.

I had a shell. I took my shell,
and all that summer day
the tube trains shuddered,
but far ... and far away ...
I heard the ocean whisper,
I heard the singing sea
hushing ... shushing ...
especially for me.

Jean Kenward

Clouds

I think
that clouds are
giant cats
purring across the sky.
Their tails fluffy
And their purring
is the wind.

Vincent Muddle (6)

10

Sunday morning

Sunday morning
    and the Sun
    bawls
    with
    his big mouth
Yachts

    paper triangles
    of white and blue
    crowd the sloping bay
    appearing motionless
    as if stuck there
    by some infant thumb

    beneath a shouting sky

    upon a painted sea

      Wes Magee

Three girls

There were three girls and they were going for
a walk along the beach till they came to a cave.
One of the girls says, 'I'm going in.'
So she goes in.

When she gets in, she sees a pile of gold
sitting on the rocks, so she thinks, 'Yippee,
gold, all for me!' and she steps forward to
pick it up and a great big voice booms out,
'I'm the ghost of Captain Cox.
All the gold stays on the rocks.'

So the girl runs out of the cave.

The second girl goes in and she sees the gold
and she thinks, 'Yippee, gold, all for me!'
and she steps forward to pick it up and the
great big voice booms out,
'I'm the ghost of Captain Cox.
All that gold stays on the rocks.'

So the girl runs out of the cave.

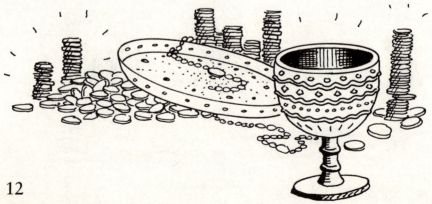

Then the third girl goes in and she sees
the gold and she thinks, 'Yippee, gold,
all for me!' and she steps forward to pick
it up and the great big voice goes,
'I'm the ghost of Captain Cox.
All that gold stays on the rocks.'
And the girl says,
'I don't care. I'm the ghost of Davy Crockett
and all that gold goes in my pocket!'
and she runs out of the cave with the gold.

Michael Rosen

Heatwave summer

The summer I was nine
I grew
A white skin bikini
With brown arms and legs
My nose peeled
And I wore
White sand stockings on my wet legs.
Got water up my nose
And sand in the sheets.
Went up and down escalators
(With sore feet)
And tried on a hundred black school shoes all size
    one-and-a-half
Ate ice-blocks at tea-time
(And grew a pink moustache)
Ate fish and chips in paper.
Kissed half-forgotten uncles
And danced in tingling seas
In a holiday heatwave.

Cathy Warry

14

Until I saw the sea

Until I saw the sea
I did not know
that wind
could wrinkle water so.

I never knew
that sun
could splinter a whole sea of blue.

Nor
did I know before
a sea breathes in and out
upon a shore.

Lilian Moore

Spray

It is a wonder foam is so beautiful.
A wave bursts in anger on a rock, broken up
in wild white sibilant spray
and falls back, drawing in its breath with rage,
with frustration how beautiful!

D. H. Lawrence

Mine

I made a sand castle.
In rolled the sea.
    'All sand castles
    belong to me –
      to me,'
said the sea.

I dug sand tunnels.
In flowed the sea.
    'All sand tunnels
    belong to me –
      to me,'
said the sea.

I saw my sand pail floating free.
I ran and snatched it from the sea.
    'My sand pail
    belongs to me –
      to ME!'

Lilian Moore

The seaside

Lying on a bed,
Sun hat on my head.
Seagulls flying,
Babies crying.
Sun lotion smelling,
Ice creams are selling.
The sun is beating,
My skin is heating.
Waves are crashing,
Castles are smashing.
Donkeys trotting,
Sea weed rotting.
What a perfect day!

Jackie Clark (13)

At the seaside

When I was down beside the sea
A wooden spade they gave to me
   To dig the sandy shore.
My holes were empty like a cup,
In every hole the sea came up,
   Till it could come no more.

Robert Louis Stevenson

Seaside

I like the seaside.
I like the sea —
I like the green wave
over me!
Slip and slither
and flow and flop ...
it never seems
to rest, or stop.
It bears the great ships
on its track
and takes them forward
and brings them back;
and in its deepest
depths, I know
luminous, bright skinned
fishes go.

The bit I paddle in's
small and sweet:
it cools my ankles
and smooths my feet.
And yet, they say
there's a great deal more,
and someone paddles
on a different shore —
a different beach
with different things,
and birds with scarlet
on their wings. ....
I guess, wherever
it might be,
I'd like the seaside.
I'd like the sea.

Jean Kenward

18

Little Barbara

Little Barbara went to Scarborough,
Just to buy a candelabra.
At the harbour a bear ate Barbara.
Don't you find that most macabre?

Colin West

The cowrie shell

My own little sea is held in a shell.
When I put it to my ear
I hear the roar of the waves
Beating on the rocks.
I hear no gulls cry
Nor any happy shouts.
All I hear are the waves
Beating on the rocks.

Yvonne Wilcock (10)

19

Sand

Sand in your fingernails
Sand between your toes
Sand in your earholes
Sand up your nose!

Sand in your sandwiches
Sand on your bananas
Sand in your bed at night
Sand in your pyjamas!

Sand in your sandals
Sand in your hair
Sand in your trousers
Sand everywhere!

John Foster

Picnic

George, lend a hand
and spread that cloth,
the sand is everywhere!
Just look at that,
you'd never think
it took hours to prepare!

WAKE UP, GRAMP!
Your food's all out,
get it while you can!
Have a lemonade before
it warms up in the sun.

What is it, Mum?
There's . . .

ham with sand,
and spam with sand,
there's chicken paste
and lamb with sand;
oranges, bananas,
lemonade or tea;
bread with sand
all spread with sand —
at least the sand comes free!
We've crisps with sand
and cake with sand —
it's grand with lunch or tea —
crunch it up,
enjoy it love,
at least we're by the sea!

Judith Nicholls

21

The sea

Take your bucket, and take your spade,
   And come to the sea with me,
Building castles upon the sand
   Is the game for you and me!
Races run with the tumbling waves,
Then rest awhile in the cool, dark caves.
Oh, the greatest joy in the summer time
   Is the sea, the sparkling sea!

E. M. Adams

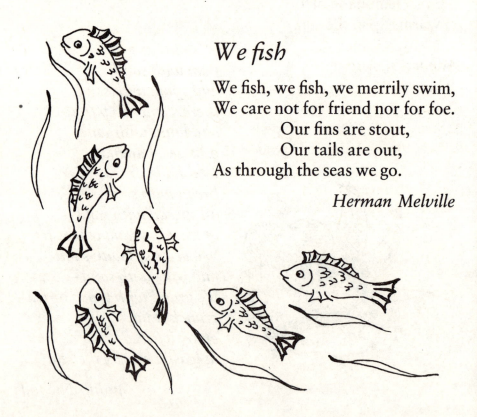

We fish

We fish, we fish, we merrily swim,
We care not for friend nor for foe.
     Our fins are stout,
     Our tails are out,
As through the seas we go.

Herman Melville

Seal

See how he dives
From rocks with a zoom!
See how he darts
Through his watery room
Past crabs and eels
And green seaweed,
Past fluffs of sandy
Minnow feed!
See how he swims
With a swerve and a twist,
A flip of the flipper,
A flick of the wrist!
Quicksilver-quick,
Softer than spray,
Down he plunges
And sweeps away;
Before you can think,
Before you can utter
Words like 'Dill pickle'
Or 'Apple butter',
Back up he swims
Past sting-ray and shark,
Out with a zoom,
A whoop, a bark;
Before you can say
Whatever you wish,
He plops at your side
With a mouthful of fish!

William Jay Smith

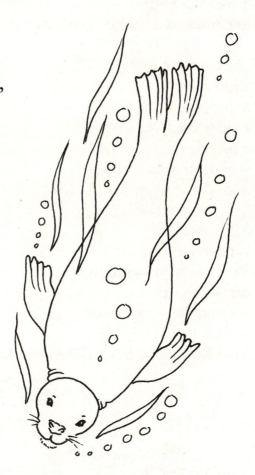

Mr O'Neil and the mermaid

A beautiful mermaid,
rainbow wet,
sat on a rock
and played her net.
She caught a shrimp,
a sprat, a trout,
and hooked a broken kettle out.

She caught a crab,
a lobster-pot,
a dripping pram,
a rusty cot,
a bicycle
with a missing wheel,
and Mr Christopher O'Neil.

Mr O'Neil
is now her friend.
You see them swimming
off Southend;
they do the backstroke
and the crawl
from Boscombe Bay to West Porthcawl.

24

They wave to people
on the pier,
then pop ashore
for chips and beer.
Or now and then
they cross to France
to taste the wine, and disco-dance.

Mrs O'Neil
was vexed, of course.
She said,
'And just to make things worse,
he's gone off
playing hide and seek,
and didn't cut the lawn last week.

'Christopher
didn't stop to pack,
just sent
a seaside postcard back,
a photo
of a Cornish Cove.
I burnt it in the kitchen stove.

'I hope we get
a west wind soon,
a howling gale,
a wild typhoon.
I hope he's tossed
by a giant wave,
and that will teach him to behave.'

Denis Manton
25

The Whale

When you are swimming do not fail
To keep a look-out for the Whale!

He has a most annoying knack
Of taking children on his back.

And when he's picked up two or three,
He whisks them off right out to sea.

Of course, at first you think it charming,
But very soon it gets alarming.

For when you say you'd like to land,
He doesn't seem to understand.

The more you beg him to go home,
The more he dashes through the foam.

He rushes on, mile after mile,
And lands you on a desert isle.

And there, until some ship appears,
You often have to stay for years.

Lord Alfred Douglas

My auntie

My auntie who lives in
Llanfairpwllgwyngyllgogerych-
　　　wyrndrobwllllantysiliogogogoch
Has asked me to stay.

But unfortunately
Llanfairpwllgwyngyllgogerych-
　　　wyrndrobwllllantysiliogogogoch
Is a long, long way away.

Will I ever go to
Llanfairpwllgwyngyllgogerych-
　　　wyrndrobwllllantysiliogogogoch?
It's difficult to say.

Colin West

27

Barefoot days

In the morning, very early,
That's the time I love to go
Barefoot where the fern grows curly
And grass is cool between each toe,
On a summer morning – O!
On a summer morning!

That is when the birds go by
Up the sunny slopes of air,
And each rose has a butterfly
Or a golden bee to wear;
And I am glad in every toe –
Such a summer morning – O!
Such a summer morning!

Rachel Field

I'm glad the sky is painted blue

I'm glad the sky is painted blue,
    And the earth is painted green,
With such a lot of nice fresh air
    All sandwiched in between.

Unknown

28

A boy's song

Where the pools are bright and deep,
Where the grey trout lies asleep,
Up the river and over the lea,
That's the way for Billy and me.

Where the blackbirds sings the latest,
Where the hawthorn blooms the sweetest,
Where the nestlings chirp and flee,
That's the way for Billy and me.

Where the mowers mow the cleanest,
Where the hay lies thick and greenest,
There to track the homeward bee,
That's the way for Billy and me.

Where the hazel bank is steepest,
Where the shadow falls the deepest,
Where the clustering nuts fall free,
That's the way for Billy and me.

This I know, I love to play,
Through the meadow, among the hay,
Up the water and over the lea,
That's the way for Billy and me.

James Hogg

29

Kite

A kite on the ground
is just paper and string
but up in the air
it will dance and will sing.
A kite in the air
will dance and will caper
but back on the ground
is just string and paper.

                    Unknown

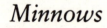

Minnows

Swarms of minnows show their little heads,
Staying their wavy bodies 'gainst the streams,
To taste the luxury of sunny beams
Tempered with coolness. How they ever wrestle
With their own sweet delight, and ever nestle
Their silver bellies on the pebbly sand.
If you but scantily hold out the hand,
That very instant not one will remain;
But turn your eye, and they are there again.

    Extract from 'I stood tiptoe on a little hill'
                    by John Keats

Here comes summer!

A curl of the hair
from the waving girls
a cascade of ringlets
dripping
      1
        2
          3
melting
ice creams
in the goldilocks sun
beams are thrown upon the sea.
A trick of clowns
on the slapstick beach.

Rebecca Heydon (10)

Upon the beach

Upon the beach
With pail and spade,
My sandy pies and wells I made.

And people passed
On every hand
And left their footprints on the sand.

Then came a wave
With the rushing tide –
And everything was washed aside.

Ilo Orleans

Davy at the seaside

1

The new day
Flooded the green bay
In a slow explosion of blue
Sky and silver sand and shimmering sea.
Boots in hand, he paddled the brilliancy
Of rippled wavelets that withdrew,
Sucking his splay grey
Feet in play.

2

It was magic – the brightness of air,
the green bay and wide arc of the sea,
with the rock-pools reflecting his stare
and a maze of wind-sculpted sand-dunes where
slum streets and the Quayside should be.

It was music – not only the sound
of the buskers outside the pub door
and the band on the pier, but the pounding of waves, the loud kids all around,
and gulls screaming shrill on the shore.

It was magic and music and motion –
there were yachts sweeping smooth in the bay
and black steamers white-plumed in mid-ocean;
and ice-cream, candy floss and commotion
as the Switchback got under way.

3

He clung
to the metal bar, clench-
ing it
TIGHT
as it swung
and wrench-
ed him
left, right
backforwards
sideways and Oh
up up up UP
(will it never touch the top?)

to a sick-
en-
ing
P
 L
  U
   N
    G
     E
and an end-
less
drop
drop
dropping
down
a dark pit-
shaft
that's
Davy's stomach.
Then a sudden
lunge
and everything slows, steadies, slides
and glides
to a
STOP.

34

4

They let him stroke
the donkeys. They
told him he could,
if he wished, stay
and see them fed
before the day
ended. Their coats
were shaggy grey.

He liked their ears
best, and the way
they curled like sea-
shells from the bay.
He stood and watched
them eat the hay,
then patted them
and went away.

5

The spent day
Drained from beach and bay
Green and silver and shimmering blue.
On prom and pier, arcade and B and B
The looped lights dimly glowed. And he could see
Stars winking at him, glimmering through
The sky's moth-eaten grey
As if in play.

Raymond Wilson

The boy fishing

I am cold and alone,
On my tree-root sitting as still as a stone.
The fish come to my net. I scorned the sun,
The voices on the road, and they have gone.
My eyes are buried in the cold pond, under
The cold, spread leaves; my thoughts are silver-wet.
I have ten stickleback, a half-day's plunder,
Safe in my jar. I shall have ten more yet.

E. J. Scovell

One-eyed Jack

One-eyed Jack, the pirate chief,
Was a terrible, fearsome ocean thief,
He wore a peg
Upon one leg;
He wore a hook –
And a dirty look!
One-eyed Jack, the pirate chief –
A terrible, fearsome ocean thief!

Unknown

That sinking feeling

He rocked the boat,
Did Ezra Shank;
These bubbles mark

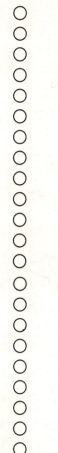

Where Ezra sank.

Unknown

Seagull

The seagull curves his wings,
the seagull turns his eyes,
Get down into the water, fish!
(if you are wise.)

The seagull slants his wings,
the seagull turns his head.
Get deep into the water, fish!
(or you'll be dead.)

Elizabeth Coatsworth

Clouds

Mackerel sky,
Mackerel sky,
Not long wet,
And not long dry.

Unknown

Joys

We may shut our eyes,
But we cannot help knowing
That skies are clear
And grass is growing;
The breeze comes whispering in our ear,
That dandelions are blossoming near,
That corn has sprouted,
That streams are flowing,
That the river is bluer than the sky,
That the robin is plastering his home hard by.

James Russell Lowell

Windsurfer

As the windsurfer flies past
He grabs hold of the wet mast
As the turned head of the board
Curves up like a Turkish sword.
The windsurfer nearly capsizes –
All his friends are criticizers.

Ahmed Barud (12)

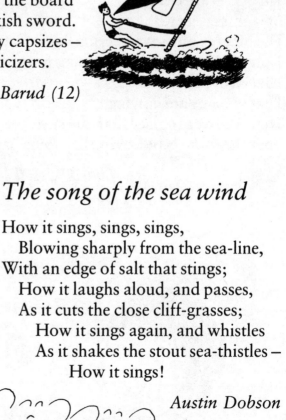

The song of the sea wind

How it sings, sings, sings,
Blowing sharply from the sea-line,
With an edge of salt that stings;
How it laughs aloud, and passes,
As it cuts the close cliff-grasses;
How it sings again, and whistles
As it shakes the stout sea-thistles –
How it sings!

Austin Dobson

The diver

I put on my aqua-lung and plunge,
Exploring, like a ship with a glass keel,
The secrets of the deep. Along my lazy road
On and on I steal! –
Over waving bushes which at a touch explode
Into shrimps, then, closing, rock to the tune of the tide;
Over crabs that vanish in puffs of sand.
Look, a string of pearls bubbling at my side
Breaks in my hand –
Those pearls were my breath! . . . Does that hollow hide
Some old Armada wreck in seaweed furled,
Crusted with barnacles, her cannon rusted,
The great San Philip? What bullion in her hold?
Pieces of eight, silver crowns, and bars of solid gold?

I shall never know. Too soon the clasping cold
Fastens on flesh and limb
And pulls me to the surface. Shivering, back I swim
To the beach, the noisy crowds, the ordinary world.

Ian Serraillier

41

Camping pie

The wind roared up
And the sea boiled up
And the clouds piled up
And the storm built up
And the tents fell down.

And the lightning flashed
And the thunder crashed
And the heavy rain splashed
And the field turned brown.

And the sleeping bags swam
With the tea-bags and spam,
Crabs crawled in the wellies
And the pillows were wet jellies
And the sweaters in the drink
Began to shrink and shrink
And every pair of woolly socks did drown.

Then the wind died down
And the sea calmed down
And the storm wound down
And the sun shone down
From a clear blue sky.

Then all the buns and beans
Sweating cheese and dripping jeans
Muddy sandwiches and babies,
Soggy dogs and damp old ladies,
Sheep in unravelled flocks
And all the limp dead socks
Were put to dry.

And the wet field gleamed
And the birds all preened
And the hot sun beamed
And everything steamed.
That's camping pie.

Julie Holder

43

Grim and gloomy

Oh, grim and gloomy,
So grim and gloomy
Are the caves beneath the sea.
Oh, rare but roomy
And bare and boomy,
Those salt sea caverns be.

Oh, slim and slimy
Or grey and grimy
Are the animals of the sea.
Salt and oozy
And safe and snoozy
The caves where those animals be.

Hark to the shuffling,
Huge and snuffling,
Ravenous, cavernous, great sea-beasts!
But fair and fabulous,
Tintinnabulous,
Gay and fabulous are their feasts.

Ah, but the queen of the sea,   Oh, rare but roomy
The querulous, perilous sea!   And bare and boomy
How the curls of her tresses   Those caverns under the sea,
The pearls on her dresses,   And grave and grandiose,
Sway and swirl in the waves,   Safe and sandiose
How cosy and dozy,   The dens of her denizens be.
How sweet ring a-rosy
Her bower in the deep-sea caves!   *James Reeves*

44

The sea

Slapping of waves on a rocky shore,
White spray flying, as foam horses ride the waves.
Swirling around above, gulls hover,
Endlessly crying the same old cry,
A cry that never changes.

Clear water, bluey-greeny shades,
Lulling of the waves on a sunny day,
Floating of the ships at harbour side,
But still the endless cry of gulls.

Crunching of pebble on a beach.
Splash splash, as waves slap the pebbles.
Thundering sounds as pebbles crash
On to the beach.
Round and smooth and hot,
As the sun shines on all day.

Lesley (11)

A postcard from Greece

The sun over here makes us browner,
after the burning wears off;
this blue kind of water is warmer
and waves are never as rough.

The flowers that grow here are brighter,
we stay up much later, to eat;
white painted houses are whiter,
the coffee is thicker, and sweet.

With sand in my undies,
cheese in the salad
and a hole in the bathroom floor,

with beds that feel harder
and days that seem longer
with things to be looking for

like donkeys and tortoises,
cats and cooked octopuses
and wine in the water to drink,

with castles on mountains
and thousands of candles
I like it in Greece, I think.

Jane Whittle

Boy with kite

I am master of my kite, and
the wind tugs against me
on blue ropes of air.
Above tasselled trees
my kite glides and swoops,
pink-and-yellow falcon surging loose
from my right fist.
White string bites
into flesh; my wrist
flexes like a falconer's.

I am dancing with my kite
heel-and-toe to earth,
body braced
against the fleet north-easter, laced
with fraying clouds.

Looking up,
lifted steeple-clear
of church and school and hill,
I am master of my world.

Phoebe Hesketh

Mountains

Mountains are today, yesterday, and for ever,
They have no likes or dislikes, no opinions –
But moods, yes. Their moods change like the weather.
They argue and quarrel, loud
With angry thunder. They rain
Rivers of stinging tears.
They hide their sulky heads in cloud
For days and days. Then suddenly, all smiles again,
One by one
Their magic cliffs stand clear
And brave, above a sea of white wave,
Under the lighthouse of the sun.

Ian Serraillier

48

Boy in bubbles

At the family picnic Dad
shook out the tablecloth, Mum
took out the sandwiches, Gran
opened the thermos flask, Uncle
told a rude joke, Cousin
told a ruder one, Uncle
smacked him, Cousin
wailed, Gran
covered her ears, Mum
ate the sandwiches, Dad said

Where's Simon?

A river runs behind the trees
Where the water licks the stone
As the leaves fly out on smoky froth
And the cold bites to the bone

Here, below the blackened weeds,
Beside the bending tree,
Among the crazed and churning foam
A boy dives: he swims, is free

Emma Payne

Hill rolling

I kind of exploded inside,
and joy shot out of me.
I began to roll down the grassy hill
I bent my knees up small, took a deep breath
and I was off.
My arms shot out sideways.
I gathered speed.
My eyes squinted
Sky and grass, dazzle and dark.

I went on forever,
My arms were covered with dents,
holes, squashed grass.
Before I knew it I was at the bottom.
The game was over.

Andrew Taylor (10)

50

Shout

Shout child, shout!
Stray from the beaten ways
And laugh out;
Sing and spring
While you can;
Can-can and dance and prance in the sun;
Son, shine and run;
Fly your voice,
Fly your kite,
Fly your life!

Keith Armstrong

51

On a blue day

On a blue day
when the brown heat
scorches the grass
and stings my legs with sweat

I go running like a fool
up the hill towards the trees
and my heart beats loudly,
like a kettle boiling dry.

I need a bucket the size of the sky
filled with cool, cascading water.

At evening
the cool air rubs my back,
I listen to the bees
working for their honey

and the sunset pours light
over my head like a waterfall.

David Harmer

The roundabout

Round and round the roundabout,
Down the 'slippery stair' –
I'm always to be found about
When circus men are there.
The music of the roundabout,
The voices in the air,
The horses as they pound about,
The boys who shout and stare –
There's such a lovely sound about
A circus or a fair.

Clive Sansom

The performing seal

Who is so proud
As not to feel
A secret awe
Before a seal
That keeps such sleek
And wet repose
While twirling candles
On his nose?

Rachel Field

At the circus

Last night the circus came to town,
And there I saw the most wonderful clown!
Oh, I saw other things as well –
A horse that danced and rang a bell,
A tiger that jumped through a burning ring,
A dog that counted and rode on a swing;
I saw elephants, lions, and bears, and seals,
And little dogs riding on big turning wheels,
And monkeys that played with a shining red ball –
But the clown was the very best thing of all!
He wore a suit of pink and black,
And hopped around with his feet in a sack;
He told funny stories and did magic tricks
With pigeons and candles and rabbits and sticks;
He juggled with balls, he sat on eight chairs
That stood on each other, piled high, in pairs;
He blew me a kiss when he waved goodbye,
And nobody clapped as loudly as I!
Oh, when can I go back to town
To see that wonderful circus clown?

Eva May

54

The tightrope walk

The band starts playing,
It's time to go,
Onwards and upwards,
And on with the show.

The crowd goes quiet as I reach the rope,
And all they do is watch and hope,
Sixty metres above the sky,
Why I do it – I don't know why.

Left foot first, followed by right,
The rope starts swaying, the crowd gets a fright.
The crowd gasp and start to call,
As I fight for balance to save my fall.

I manage to hold it, the act's gone well,
Nobody injured, nobody fell.
I've reached the ground safely. I'm the star of the show,
The clowns come on next, that's the circus, you know.

Phillip John Hoskin (11)

Radi

Radi was a circus lion,
Radi was a woman hater.
Radi had a lady trainer,
Radiator.

Unknown

Trapeze artist

A sea of smiling faces
Waves dizzily below.
The sawdust appears, uncertainly
For half a second.
Someone's glittering costume
Looms before her ...
She grabs it.
The mouths below cheer.
Limbs entwined,
She swings to the safety
Of a creaking, wooden parapet –
Flushed red, but
Smiling.

Kate Quinn (12)

Merry-go-round

Red horse!...green!...the Cambridge horse,
Blue as the summer sky...
People call, organs bawl,
The cavalry thunders by.

White horse!...grey!...the chestnut horse...
Fierce as the wind and fast,
With flowing manes and plunging hooves
The steeds go charging past.

Red horse!...green!...the Cambridge horse,
Blue as the summer sky...
The coloured music churns the air,
The circling horses fly.

All day long on the crowded Heath
They run their endless race;
The sun goes down, the flares come out,
But still the hunters chase.

Red horse!...green!...the Cambridge horse...
Across the star-pricked sky,
Into the night, the ball of white,
The moon goes whirling by.

Slower the riders rise and fall,
Slower their friends pursue –
White...grey...chestnut...black...
Red...green...blue...

Clive Sansom

Fun fair

Riding high then riding low,
On our merry way we go,
Music blaring – lights ablaze,
Happy, happy, fun filled days.
Candy floss and lemonade,
Phew! Let's find a little shade.
Hoopla – darts to test your eye,
Shall we have another try?
Pocket money almost spent,
Goodness knows just where it went;
Having too much fun to care,
How we love it at the fair!

Philip F. Williams

All for an ice-cream

'Mum, can I have an ice-cream?'
'Go ask your dad.'
'Dad, can I have an ice-cream?'
'Go ask your mum.'
'But I've just asked her and she told me to ask you.'
'Well tell her that I've told you to ask her.'
'Mum, dad's just told me to tell you that you've got to tell
    me if I can have an ice.'
'Oh well I suppose you can but go ask your dad for 10p.'
'Right.'
'Dad, can I have 10p for an ice-cream?'
'I haven't got 10p.'
'Oh come on dad you haven't looked yet and oh hurry the
    van'll go soon.'
'Let's have a look then, ah, there you are.'
'Thanks dad, Ohh!'
'What's matter now?'
'The van's gone.'

Karen Jackson

Uncle William

I stayed with you once
in your tiny church-lane cottage
with the outside pump, the velvet cloth
and sing-songs cramped around the piano.

With black-fringed stumps of fingers,
braces, ample paunch,
you could have been
miner, dustman, sweep –
but no; village blacksmith
fitted best that village scene.

I remember strong green soap,
tin bowls of icy water for the morning wash;
my aunt's night-calling for the cat
across still hedgerows and the cobbled lane,
a shared bed with spoiling cousins,
Billy Bunter by oil lamp at forbidden hours
and orange moths against the darkened pane.

Uncle William. Dead now;
the blacksmith and the cottage gone.
No cobbled lane but just a road now,
a road my aunt must tread alone.

Judith Nicholls

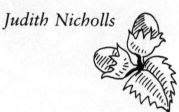

Over the fields

Over the fields where the cornflowers grow,
Over the fields where the poppies blow,
Over the stile there's a way we know –
    Down to a rustling wood!

Over the fields where the daisies grow,
Over the bank where the willows blow,
Over the bridge there's a way we know –
    Down to a rippling brook!

Over the hills where the rainbows go,
Where golden gorse and brambles grow,
Over the hills there's a way we know –
    Down to a rolling sea!

Adeline White

Rock pool

Rock pool, rock pool,
See the sand guzzle
The sour sea.
Each drip of water,
Tasteless and dry.
A swirl of sand
Rubs between my toes,
Worms wriggling.

Faint echoes of ships' horns
Blowing
And the rock pool humming.
A small crab,
Its legs long, thin;
Its eyes,
Size of melon pips.
I touch the crab's shell,
Hard but breakable.
A pebble lies crushed,
Smashed against the tide's
Pestle and mortar.
And now
The pebbles are the sands.

Michelle Saunders (13)

Let's hear it for the limpet

If there's one animal that isn't a wimp, it
Is the limpet.

Let me provide an explanation
For my admiration.

To start with, it's got two thousand tiny teeth
Beneath

Its comical conical-hat-shaped, greeny-grey shell:
A tongue as well

That rasps the delicate seaweed through its front door:
What's more –

And this is what gives me the greatest surprise –
Two bright eyes

Indoors at the end of long tentacles poking out, which
Twitch.

But its funniest feature by far is its foot
That's put

Straight down to clamp it fast to the rock.
(Gulls knock,

You see, at the shell to try and winkle it off
For scoff.)

Kit Wright

Real life

'Yes,' thought John
his eyes gleaming with excitement
as he looked round the ancient Inn
on the edge of the moors
that was connected to
otherwise inaccessible St Peter's Cove
which had once been a haunt of smugglers
by a secret underground passage
from his bedroom
and which his strange Aunt Lucy
had rented to his mother and father
and Uncle David for
the whole summer holidays,
'Yes this looks just the sort
of place for an adventure but
that kind of thing
only happens in books.'
And he was right.

Gareth Owen

Camels

The sea gets rough
Getting higher and higher
Multiplying like thousands of camels
Marching across a blue desert.

Steven Jackson (11)

Hot day

It was too hot to play,
  So I lay down.
I listened to the crickets,
  Lazing on a stone,
Singing drowsily as they dozed.

The lizard lay basking
  Motionless, without a wink
Of an eye;
  His skin shining
Like a diamond.

Slowly the cows moved
  As they grazed;
A sudden breeze
  Rippled the grass.

The daisy's eye
  Stared up,
To where its golden eye
  Met the golden eye
Of the sun.

> *Jacqueline Hamer*

65

Three little girls

Three little girls were sitting on a rail,
    Sitting on a rail,
    Sitting on a rail;
Three little girls were sitting on a rail,
On a fine hot day in September.

What did they talk about that fine day,
    That fine day,
    That fine day?
What did they talk about that fine day,
That fine hot day in September?

The crows and the corn they talked about,
    Talked about,
    Talked about;
But nobody knows what was said by the crows,
On that fine hot day in September.

Kate Greenaway

August afternoon

Where shall we go?
   What shall we play?
What shall we do
   On a hot summer day?

We'll sit in the swing.
   Go low. Go high.
And drink lemonade
   Till the glass is dry.

One straw for you,
   One straw for me,
In the cool green shade
   Of the walnut tree.

Marion Edey

The hardest thing to do in the world

The hardest thing to do in the world
is stand in the hot sun
at the end of a long queue for ice creams
watching all the people who've just bought theirs
coming away from the queue
giving their ice creams their very first lick.

Michael Rosen

Over my toes

Over my toes
goes
the soft sea wash
see the sea wash
the soft sand slip
see the sea slip
the soft sand slide
see the sea slide
the soft sand slap
see the sea slap
the soft sand wash
over my toes.

Michael Rosen

Learning to swim

Today I am
dolphin-over-the-waves,
roach and stickleback,
silver mermaid,
turning tide,
ribbon-weed
or sprat.

Water drifts through my mind;
I twist, I glide,
leave fear behind in sand,
wander a land
of turtle, minnow, seal
where whale is king.
Today – I swim!

Judith Nicholls

The s-s-s-s-s-seashore

Simon and Susan and Stephen
heard the swish of the surf,
sniffed the sweet scent
of seaweed, and stared at shrimps
shifting in still pools.

Susan and Stephen and Simon
spied children swimming and sunbathing.
They saw a starfish
stuck on a sandcastle
and searched for shells on the shore.

Stephen and Simon and Susan,
those silly stupids,
got stuck in squelchy, sloshy,
sucking sand as seagulls screeched
in the sun-struck sky.

Wes Magee

69

Frolic

The children were shouting together
  And racing along the sands,
A glimmer of dancing shadows,
  A dove-like flutter of hands.

The stars were shouting in heaven,
  The sun was chasing the moon,
The game was the same as the children's,
  They danced to the self-same tune.

The whole of the world was merry,
  One joy from the vale to the height,
Where the blue woods of twilight encircled
  The lovely lawns of the light.

A.E.

O to sail

O to sail in a ship,
To leave this steady unendurable land,
To leave the tiresome sameness of the streets, the sidewalks
  and the houses,
To leave you, O you solid motionless land, and entering a
  ship,
To sail and sail and sail!

Walt Whitman

70

What has happened to Lulu?

What has happened to Lulu, mother?
  What has happened to Lu?
There's nothing in her bed but an old rag-doll
  And by its side a shoe.

Why is her window wide, mother,
  The curtain flapping free,
And only a circle on the dusty shelf
  Where her money-box used to be?

Why do you turn your head, mother,
  And why do the tear-drops fall?
And why do you crumple that note on the fire
  And say it is nothing at all?

I woke to voices late last night,
  I heard an engine roar.
Why do you tell me the things I heard
  Were a dream and nothing more?

I heard somebody cry, mother,
  In anger or in pain,
But now I ask you why, mother,
  You say it was a gust of rain.

Why do you wander about as though
  You don't know what to do?
What has happened to Lulu, mother?
  What has happened to Lu?

Charles Causley

Wish you were here

Midbay-on-Sea
August 9

Dear Kevin,
      Thought I'd drop a line
with kind regards to everyone.
Wish you were here to share the fun.
Arrived in rain last Saturday,
And will it stop? No blooming way –
Looks like going on for weeks.
Our caravan has fifteen leaks:
It's saturated all our gear.
Kevin, love, wish you were here.
Dad wishes that he hadn't come,
Yesterday he hurt his thumb:
Trapped it in a folding chair –
You should have heard him curse and swear!
He says the beer down here's no good.
The beach has got no sand – just mud;
And what's between us and the sea?
You'll never guess – a cemetery;
When I'm out walking with the pup
I go that way – it cheers me up.
My new swimsuit gave Mum a fit:
She says there's not enough of it.
Closing now, Kev, I'm off to bed,
Think I've got flu, I feel half-dead.
Hoping from this exciting whirl,
You're not out with some other girl.
Much love from Misery-on-Sea,
Wish you were here,
      Your girl friend,
         G.   *Eric Finney*

Have you heard the sun singing?

Have you ever heard the sun in the sky
Man have you heard it?
Have you heard it break the black of night
Man have you heard it?
Have you heard it shouting its song, have you heard
It scorch up the air like a phoenix bird,
Have you heard the sun singing?

John Smith

What is the Sun?

the Sun is an orange dinghy
    sailing across a calm sea

it is a gold coin
    dropped down a drain in Heaven

the Sun is a yellow beach ball
    kicked high into the summer sky

it is a red thumb-print
    on a sheet of pale blue paper

the Sun is a milk bottle's gold top
    floating in a puddle

Wes Magee

Seaweed

A myriad tides have foamed
    And myriad moons been lit
While this brown weed was made
    And sea-stones clothed in it.

All time, and this vast world's
    Strong tides, sun, moon, and air
Have laboured to display
    Eternal autumn there!

William Jeffrey

Racing the tide

With long tail flowing and dark coat glowing,
His eyes roll white in the bright moonlight.
His pounding hooves thump on the smooth sands,
He leaps a bush and with grace he lands.
He flicks his tail, then he twitches an ear,
He kicks up his hooves but he shows no fear.

His nostrils flare with excitement I share,
In the dark night, his mane gleams bright.
He gallops through waves, racing the tide,
Arching his neck, his head held with pride.
He enters a cave, his strides echo on,
I quickly pursue him, but he is gone!

Jennifer Digby (13)

The pool in the rock

In this water, clear as air,
Lurks a lobster in its lair.
Rock-bound weed sways out and in,
Coral-red, and bottle green.
Wondrous pale anemones
Stir like flowers in a breeze.
Fluted scallop, whelk in shell,
And the prowling mackerel.
Winged with snow the sea-mews ride
The brine-keen wind; and far and wide
Sounds on the hollow thunder of the tide.

Walter de la Mare

The sea

Behold the wonders of the mighty deep,
Where crabs and lobsters learn to creep,
And little fishes learn to swim,
And clumsy sailors tumble in.

Unknown

Tell me, tell me, Sarah Jane

Tell me, tell me, Sarah Jane,
   Tell me, dearest daughter,
Why are you holding in your hand
   A thimbleful of water?
Why do you hold it to your eye
   And gaze both late and soon
From early morning light until
   The rising of the moon?

Mother, I hear the mermaids cry,
   I hear the mermen sing,
And I can see the sailing-ships
   All made of sticks and string.
And I can see the jumping fish,
   The whales that fall and rise
And swim about the waterspout
   That swarms up to the skies.

Tell me, tell me, Sarah Jane,
   Tell your darling mother,
Why do you walk beside the tide
   As though you loved none other?
Why do you listen to a shell
   And watch the billows curl,
And throw away your diamond ring
   And wear instead the pearl?

Mother I hear the water
    Beneath the headland pinned,
And I can see the sea-gull
    Sliding down the wind.
I taste the salt upon my tongue
    As sweet as sweet can be.

Tell me, my dear, whose voice you hear?

It is the sea, the sea.

                    Charles Causley

Stony

We found this secret beach
Of sea-smooth stones last year:
What fun we had there!
We flung them out to sea at first
Over the running tide,
Your lazy throws
Always the winners
No matter how hard I tried.
Then we bombed blobs
Of seaweed
With nearly fist-sized stones:
At hits and near-misses
Gave cheers or groans,
Till, leaning against two boulders,
Arms round each other's shoulders
We listened to shifting stones
In the tug and suck of the sea;
Last year, you and me.

This year, remembering,
I walked the beach alone
And everything was cold
And grey as stone.

Eric Finney

Old Man Ocean

Old Man Ocean, how do you pound
Smooth glass, rough stones round?
  Time and the tide and the wild waves rolling
  Night and the wind and the long grey dawn.

Old Man Ocean, what do you tell,
What do you sing in the empty shell?
  Fog and the storm and the long bell tolling,
  Bones in the deep and the brave men gone.

Russell Hoban

The lighthouse keeper

I met the lighthouse
  keeper's wife,
His nephew, niece,
  and daughter;
His uncle and his
  auntie too,
When I went 'cross
  the water.

I met the lighthouse
  keeper's son,
His father and his
  mother;
His grandpa and his
  grandma too,
His sister and his
  brother.

I met the lighthouse
  keeper's mate,
Who, running out
  of patience,
Told me, 'The keeper's
  gone ashore
To round up more
  relations.'

Colin West

80

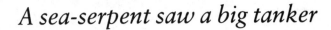

A sea-serpent saw a big tanker

A sea-serpent saw a big tanker,
Bit a hole in her side and then sank her.
    It swallowed the crew
    In a minute or two,
And then picked its teeth with the anchor.

Unknown

The Sword-fish

The Sword-fish is an awful brute,
He tears your hair out by the root.

And when you're bathing in the sea,
He leaps upon you suddenly

And if you get out on the sand,
He sometimes follows you inland.

Lord Alfred Douglas

81

Fishes' evening song

Flip flop,
Flip flap,
Slip slap,
Lip lap;
Water sounds,
Soothing sounds.
We fan our fins
As we lie
Resting here
Eye to eye.
Water falls
Drop by drop,
Plip plop,
Drip drop.
Plink plunk,
Splash splish;
Fish fins fan,
Fish tails swish,
Swush, swash, swish.
This we wish . . .
Water cold,
Water clear,
Water smooth,
Just to soothe
Sleepy fish.

Dahlov Ipcar

Little fish

The tiny fish enjoy themselves
in the sea.
Quick little splinters of life,
their little lives are fun to them
in the sea.

D. H. Lawrence

The lighthouse

What I remember best about
my holiday was how, each night,
the lighthouse kept sweeping my bedroom
with its clean, cool ray of light.

I lay there, tucked up in the blankets,
and suddenly the lighthouse shone:
a switched on torch that stabbed the night
like a murderer and moved on.

Then back it came, out of the dark,
and swung round, as in some fixed plan:
the light of the lighthouse – opening,
folding, and closing like a fan.

Raymond Wilson

The dolphin

On a beach in the morning
The sea green and blue
A young child was resting:
The same age as you.

From a spot near a towel
A whispering came
Like a rustle of leaves
Or a voice in a dream.

Where the ripples were circling
A dolphin appeared
And said, 'Come down with me.'
And then – DISappeared.

The child entered softly
and reached the sea-floor
And saw not a sign
Of the golden sea-shore.

There were molluscs in sea-shells
Anemones too,
And more fish than the child
Had observed in the zoo.

On the back of the dolphin
The child wished and watched
How the fish gather round
As the fish-eggs are hatched.

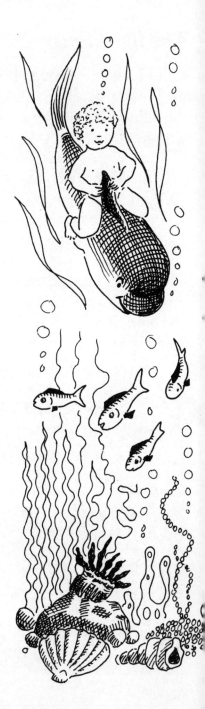

Faster and faster
The dolphin progressed
And they passed near to China
As they streaked from the West.

And then there were goldfish
As large as your knee,
And twenty-five pandas
Asleep by the sea.

In India fish had
The most wonderful marks
(But they missed out Australia
Because of the sharks).

At the end of the journey
They were back near the beach
When they talked of their trip
With bubbles for speech.

Then the child swam back strongly
to the spot on the sand
And covered up eyes
with the back of a hand.

In an hour the child woke up
In bed, it would seem.
Do you think that it happened
Or was it a dream?

Alan Bold

Holidays at home

There was a family who, every year,
Would go abroad, sometimes to Italy,
Sometimes to France. The youngest did not dare
To say, 'I much prefer to stay right here.'

You see, abroad there were no slot-machines,
No bright pink rock with one name going through it,
No rain, no boarding-houses, no baked beans,
No landladies, and no familiar scenes.

And George, the youngest boy, so longed to say,
'I don't *like* Greece. I don't like all these views,
I don't like having fierce sun every day,
And, most of all, I just detest the way

The food is cooked – that garlic and that soup,
Those strings of pasta, and no cakes at all.'
The family wondered why George seemed to droop
And looked just like a thin hen in a coop.

They never guessed why when they said, 'Next year
We can't afford abroad, we'll stay right here,'
George looked so pleased and soon began to dream
Of piers, pink rock, deep sand, and Devonshire cream.

Elizabeth Jennings

Farewell to the farm

The coach is at the door at last;
The eager children, mounting fast
And kissing hands, in chorus sing:
'Goodbye, goodbye, to everything!

'To house and garden, field and lawn,
The meadow-gates we swang upon,
To pump and stable, tree and swing,
Goodbye, goodbye, to everything!

'And fare you well for evermore,
O ladder at the hayloft door,
O hayloft where the cobwebs cling,
Goodbye, goodbye, to everything!'

Crack goes the whip, and off we go;
The trees and houses smaller grow;
Last, round the woody turn we swing;
'Goodbye, goodbye, to everything!'

Robert Louis Stevenson

Journey home

I remember the long homeward ride, begun
By the light that slanted in from the level sun;
And on the far embankment, in sunny heat,
Our whole train's shadow travelling, dark and complete.

A farmer snored. Two loud gentlemen spoke
Of the cricket and news. The pink baby awoke
And gurgled awhile. Till slowly out of the day
The last light sank in glimmer and ashy-grey.

I remember it all; and dimly remember, too,
The place where we changed – the dark trains lumbering
   through;
The refreshment-room, the crumbs and the slopped tea;
And the salt on my face, not of tears, not tears, but the sea.

Our train at last! Said Father, 'Now tumble in!
It's the last lap home!' And I wondered what 'lap' could
   mean;
But the rest is all lost, for a huge drowsiness crept
Like a yawn upon me; I leant against Mother and slept.

John Walsh

88

Poems to paddle in

When you're a whole long year away
From yacht and lighthouse, cliff and shore,
When life and work are a sickening bore
And you're back at home and school once more,
    Hold on to your holiday.

It's true that memories grow thin
And the only rockpool left behind
Is the ebbing rockpool in your mind –
Yet a book of verse will help you find
    Poems to paddle in!

Raymond Wilson

Index of Authors

Index of first lines

Acknowledgements

The compiler and publishers would like to thank the following people for giving permission to include in this anthology material which is their copyright. The publishers have made every effort to trace copyright holders. If we have inadvertently omitted to acknowledge anyone we should be most grateful if this could be brought to our attention for correction at the first opportunity.

Alan Bold: 'The dolphin' from *A Very First Poetry Book*, ed. John Foster, 1984.

Cadbury Ltd., for permission to reprint the following poems, which first appeared in Cadbury's Children's Poetry books:
'Windsurfer' by Ahmed Barud; 'The seaside' by Jackie Clark; 'Racing the tide' by Jennifer Digby; 'Clouds' by Vincent Muddle; 'Trapeze artist' by Kate Quinn.

Charles Causley: 'What has happened to Lulu?'; 'Tell me, tell me, Sara Jane'. From *Collected Poems* (Macmillan).

Walter de la Mare: 'The pool in the rock'. The Literary Trustees of Walter de la Mare and The Society of Authors as their representative.

Max Fatchen: 'Holiday'. © Max Fatchen 1987. By permission of John Johnson Ltd.

Eric Finney: 'Wish you were here'. © Eric Finney. 'Stony' from *Another First Poetry Book*, ed. John Foster.

John L. Foster: 'Sand'. © 1988 by John Foster, from *Another First Poetry Book* published by Oxford University Press, reprinted by permission of the author.

David Harmer: 'On a blue day'. © David Harmer, from *A 5th Poetry Book*, ed. John Foster.

Phoebe Hesketh: 'Boy with kite', from *Netting the Sun: New and Collected Poems*, E. Wittenham. 1989.

Julie Holder: 'Camping pie', from *A 3rd Poetry Book* compiled by John Foster, published by Oxford University Press.

William Jeffrey: 'Seaweed', from *A Second Scottish Poetry Book*. (1985)

Elizabeth Jennings: 'Holidays at home' from *The Secret Brother* (Macmillan).

Jean Kenward: 'Seaside'; 'Shell'; © Jean Kenward.